INFRA-APPAREL

INFRA-APPAREL

Richard Martin and Harold Koda

Photographs by Neil Selkirk

THE METROPOLITAN MUSEUM OF ART, NEW YORK

Distributed by Harry N. Abrams, Inc., New York

This volume has been published in conjunction with the exhibition "Infra-Apparel," held at The Metropolitan Museum of Art from April 1, 1993, to August 8, 1993.

The exhibition is made possible by

NATORI

Published by The Metropolitan Museum of Art, New York
Copyright © 1993 by The Metropolitan Museum of Art, New York

John P. O'Neill, Editor in Chief
Barbara Burn, Project Supervisor
Barbara Cavaliere, Editor
Peter Antony, Production

Library of Congress Cataloging-in-Publication Data
Martin, Richard (Richard Harrison)
Infra-apparel / by Richard Martin and Harold Koda.
p.   cm.
A catalog to an exhibition at the Costume Institute of the Metropolitan Museum of Art.
Includes bibliographical references.
ISBN 0-87099-676-2 (Pbk.).—ISBN 0-8109-6430-9 (Abrams)
1. Underwear—History—Exhibitions.   I. Koda, Harold.
II. Costume Institute (New York, N.Y.)   III. Title.
GT2073.M35   1993
391′.42′0747471—dc20   93-9564
CIP

Composition by U.S. Lithograph, typographers, New York
Printed and bound by Meridian Printing Company,
East Greenwich, Rhode Island

Cover: Fendi, *Corset bathing suit,* spring/summer 1991
Frontispiece: French, *Robe volante,* ca. 1735–40
Page 5: Gabrielle Chanel, *Evening ensemble,* 1939
Page 6: Josie Natori, left: *Slip dress,* fall/winter 1990–91;
right: *Baby doll dress,* spring/summer 1990

Art Direction/Design by Yolanda Cuomo

CONTENTS

FOREWORD

———

The Costume Institute of The Metropolitan Museum of Art has one of the finest and most comprehensive collections of costume in the world, dating from the eighteenth century to the present day. We are extremely pleased to welcome to The Costume Institute Richard Martin, Curator, and Harold Koda, Associate Curator, who assumed their official duties on January 1, 1993. However, as one might imagine, long before that date they were nurturing, indeed planning, their first exhibition at the Metropolitan, *Infra-Apparel*.

This exhibition heralds a series of thematic shows conceived to examine various elements in the history of costume, with selections culled primarily from the Museum's own collections. Thus reaffirming the Museum's commitment to collecting and to the care and display of costume, these installations will offer substantial displays year round as well as an extraordinary opportunity to evaluate and appreciate the evolution of costume over the last three centuries.

The depth and scope of our collections should provide the curators with an inexhaustible source of challenging subjects and inspiration for exhibitions, research, publications, and teaching programs far into the next century. It is therefore with much pleasure and great expectation that we offer *Infra-Apparel*, the first in an exciting series of projects envisioned by our new curators, Mr. Martin and Mr. Koda.

Philippe de Montebello
Director
The Metropolitan Museum of Art

Page 9: Jean Paul Gaultier,
"Express Yourself" ensemble,
1990, courtesy Madonna

8

INTRODUCTION

———

Infra-Apparel, the exhibition and the book that accompanies it, has had to search for its own name. There is not a single word or descriptive phrase that fully signifies the phenomenon we seek to describe and the argument we are attempting to make. It is simplistic to offer our argument as structure disclosed, inside appearing on the outside, or externalization as a function of familiarity, yet all of these are approximations of parts of the argument. Jean Baudrillard has argued that fashion is exceptional within culture in its proclivity to propagate signs, some of substantive, others of scant meaning. The larger significance of the observation we make in *Infra-Apparel* is the transaction that occurred from the eighteenth century to the present between the intimate and personal and the social and public. Without consistent evolution, but with a fascinating persistence, clothing has sought to convey elements of boudoir privacy to the public domain. Moreover, underwear can be perceived as the required interface between the body and clothing, but it can also constitute clothing's ultimate seduction. Function and finery meet with oppositional intensity in underwear and lingerie. Clothing is a principal means by which we negotiate between private and public realms.

It was once fashionable to frame the reasoning of the history and psychology of dress in the manner of self-expression and social contract as a kind of implicit dialectic. Individual choice would be held in contention against the responsibility of dress to register social relationships. Zones such as time of day, other persons present, formality or informality, and social class and circumstance have generally distinguished appropriate clothing for individuals. Costume surely does more than externalize itself; it brings the individual to the community, allowing interchange but also setting forth some initial elements of that dialogue. *Infra-Apparel* suggests, of course, that there are elements inherent in dress that become expressive as part of the personal to public exchange.

In our time, public and private worlds collide prominently and even painfully in technology, celebrity, social action, and decorum. We may be profoundly discomforted by that which we had expected to remain intimate instead becoming public. The history of costume has had its revelations and has violated its own protocol. One generation's lingerie may become another generation's visible clothing. The tacit morphology of clothing in one era can become the declared armature of dress in another. Costume's structure can be built and unbuilt in our daily witness in the act of dressing, but it can also be presented in macro-attestation as clothing self-consciously analyzes itself. Art has played a significant role in granting us accustomed spectatorship to the spectrum of nudity, deshabille, the process of dressing in the levee and its more bourgeois toilette, and of dress. As Anne Hollander has argued in *Seeing Through Clothes*, art has served as a visualizing process, a template for our seeing even in quotidian circumstances.

Of course, the argument for *Infra-Apparel* is based in the belief that clothing is important. In the same manner in which art history is certain that visual culture bears upon civilization in substantial ways, we are confident that dress bears culture and bares culture.

SEDUCTIVE STRATA

The Emergence of Underwear

Clothing is not the organism that a natural form might be, but it is nonetheless capable of simile with, let us say, the onion in its layered development, especially in the West. For reasons of laminated protection such as covering the body from the abrasion of any rough outer garment, dress conventionally has had an underlayer largely hidden from view but yielding service in heating or ventilating the body and in protecting tender human skin from tougher skin or fabrics. Similarly, an interface protected the clothing so that the finest materials could be used in garments—at least prior to the modern notion of fashion change—for generations.

But art and life have conspired to reveal those inner layers, which sometimes come through to the exterior, as in men's shirts pulled through the finer materials of jackets especially slashed for aperture or in the innermost layer and shifts for women that served their practical purpose but were visible in decorated and embroidered borders and edges. One might also imagine that the delectation of the clothing revealed was only the complement to the pleasures of clothing concealed, the enchantment of a rich detail or pretty passage that is a private poetry in the midst of underwear's vernacular. If there was a garment one step removed from the fig leaf, it was the shift, the basic form suspended from the shoulders with a wide opening for the neck and passage over the head, but extending down to the legs to protect outer garments from the body and to afford modesty and some control of temperature and possible friction against the body.

Inadvertent appearances of underwear have probably always occurred. In the nineteenth century, flirtatious views of underwear passed from voyeuristic accounts to a stan-

Page 12: Attributed to Élisabeth Vigée-Lebrun, *Marie Antoinette,* ca. 1783

dard strategy of entertainment and seduction. But there are also instances of the self-conscious emergence of underwear to external layer and visibility.

Perhaps the most substantive and indicative instance of the manifestation of underwear is Marie Antoinette's appearance in a cotton shift or *chemise à la reine*. In a painting of about 1783 attributed to Élisabeth Vigée-Lebrun, Marie Antoinette sits for her portrait in the new style that she unequivocally launched or sanctioned. If the *chemise à la reine* was an expression of personal caprice and freedom in the years immediately before the French Revolution, it was a gesture of its time, corresponding in profound ways with the philosophies of naturalism of Rousseau-inspired returns to nature as well as being a welcome détente literally and figuratively for French women. The human body, reformists argued for nearly a century of gradually increasing freedom, is not constricted in nature, nor is its ideal to be found in a shape determined by aesthetic idealism but instead by the configurations of women. No Lady Godiva, but no philosopher either, Marie Antoinette made her dress decision as if discarding the outer layers of body shaping and rich materials. The decision made in dress became a decision of imagery as well. The *chemise à la reine*, which Aileen Ribeiro in *Dress and Morality* calls "*the* sartorial success story of the 1780s," was a clothing of emancipation from the most rigid tradition of court dress. It is, of course, ironic that these startlingly democratic and liberated matters of dress anticipate the Revolution and emanate from the Court. There was, however, criticism of the new style. Some called the diaphanous chemise the dress of prostitutes and unsuitable for public presentation. But such deprecating refutation was patently thwarted by the immediate and emphatic creation of the iconography of the Vigée-Lebrun portrait, asserting the newly "appropriate" form of attire.

For the queen to appear and to be given image in what was heretofore a kind of undress required a transmogrification of the apparel's significance. If the chemise was only a hidden layer, there would be no reason for it to appear externally. The Age of Reason demanded accountability of clothing. The chemise could be justified as primary dress and as the most unconstrained garment. Further, it returned modern Europe to an

Page 15: Follower of Jacques-Louis David, *Portrait of a Young Woman in White,* ca. 1800

ancient model of dress. Dress from the 1780s into the first decade of the nineteenth century emulated the dress of the Greek democracy and the Roman world, thus more than fortuitously aligning itself with the yearnings for and simulations of those cultures as exemplary for the modern state. Wearing the *chemise à la reine*, the modern woman might specifically emulate Marie Antoinette, but in larger historical and more visually inferential terms, she stepped into the world of Jacques-Louis David paintings and from there into the voluptuous drapery of classical art. Could one prove the salacious misappropriation of undergarments to external clothing, if there were at least the equivocal similarity —perhaps what Robert Rosenblum, in his 1975 book, *Modern Painting and the Northern Romantic Tradition: Friedrich to Rothko*, describes as coincidental visual similarity, pseudomorphism—with a desired and intellectually cognate and compelling historical dress? Reason and the good health and good sense of dress played a role in justifying the *chemise à la reine* as these motives would prompt dress reform throughout the nineteenth century, but the most persuasive aspect of its acceptance, surpassing any opprobrium attached to underwear, was the suggestive beauty and referenced association of its appearance. To those who saw the emergence of underwear in this instance as exposure alone, the act was tainted by commonness or lubricity. To those who saw the neoclassical restitution and resemblance, the act was noble. But if Jacques-Louis David's Madame Récamier was, in fact, dressed in the manner of the heroines who had peopled the artist's allegorical *tableaux d'histoire* of the eighteenth century, Madame Récamier's clothing of about 1800 was significantly sanctioned by the past, more comparable and more compelling than base provocation. In fact, the style might have persisted longer had not the First Empire taken the concept to some excess by some women wearing the chemise soaked in water to simulate more fully the cling of classical drapery. The frozen stillness of statues became the pernicious chill of women shivering and exposed to illness because they were following the fashion of wearing damp clothing on cool nights. Pygmalion ultimately surrendered to pragmatism, but not before the sanctions of sculpture and classicism had allowed for radical change in dress.

Page 16: American. *Dress,* 1799–1800

A little more than a hundred years after the fashion of the *chemise à la reine*, its success was reiterated by the intimate appearance and quick public resolution of the Fortuny tea gown. The pleated silk gown, the Delphos form that took its name from its profound resemblance to the drapery of a classical sculpture in Delphi called the *Charioteer*, so convincingly emulated a classical type that its initial role as dress reserved for the intimate tea and colloquy among women was extended to dress for evening, including occasions involving contact with men. The extended use of the Fortuny gown was also not without its first range of critics deploring the use that seems to have come in its popularity with women of the theater, who first wore the gown with cloaks and dressing robes, rather in the manner of the eighteenth century. Fortuny created, as had the *chemise à la reine* more than a hundred years before, a *Magic Mountain* classicism, made flesh and blood in the sensuality it ascribed to the classical model. To be sure, the Fortuny gown was richer in reference, detailing (generally with exquisite Murano beads to create an equivalent of outline), and textile to the chemise as an underwear interface, but the untailored structure was of the same heritage, one which Fortuny would have known not only from a Western chemise or shift but also from external garments of North Africa, the Middle East, and Asia. The caftans, djellabahs, long jackets, and other coverings created by Fortuny provided some modest accompaniment to the Delphos, but the short jacket was often favored, still revealing the Delphos as a kind of lingerie-like intimacy.

Two twentieth-century dresses are the inevitable result of undergarments; they emanate from the shift, though in its more decorated form. The Baby Doll dress of the 1950s took advantage of a moment of short skirts to drop a lingerie-inspired cone over the shoulders, which swings out from the body with a luxury of motion and the seductiveness of lingerie and nightwear. At first glance, it might have been difficult to be sure whether the apparel was loungewear or evening wear. Later, the slip dress obviated underwear by allowing lacy elements of the dress to reveal the body in ways that were irreconcilable with a full undergarment. Geoffrey Beene's lace gyrations around the body in a slip dress make the dress very like a slip, enjoying the luxury of technique, the fineness of feeling, and the sensuousness of intimate apparel. Taking inspiration from the slip dress in the 1980s, innerwear designers have found common ground with the designers of evening wear, both making garments that have delicacy along with public presence.

Of course, when intimate apparel emerges, it may seem to lose its intimacy. A significant impulse to the refined decoration of underwear in the nineteenth century was its ability to share appearance with outer clothing. Once undergarments came to frequent and decorous exposure—beginning probably, for the modern world, not with the *chemise à la reine* but with the earlier *robe volante* that had already traversed from boudoir into public zones, due in large part to dressing ritual and imagery—they began increasingly to share a vocabulary of decoration and design with other apparel. Thus, there is no constant or consistent practice of bringing undergarments into the public view, but rather a more subtle and shifting process in which some specific attribute of clothing might attach itself to intimate apparel and in which devices of intimate apparel might yield expanded and exposed service to the layer of clothing that may yet all but hide their source beneath an outer layer.

Page 21: Alfred Stieglitz,
Mrs. Selma Schubart
(Stieglitz's sister Selma), 1907

Pages 22–23: Mariano Fortuny,
Delphos dresses, ca. 1920 – ca. 1950

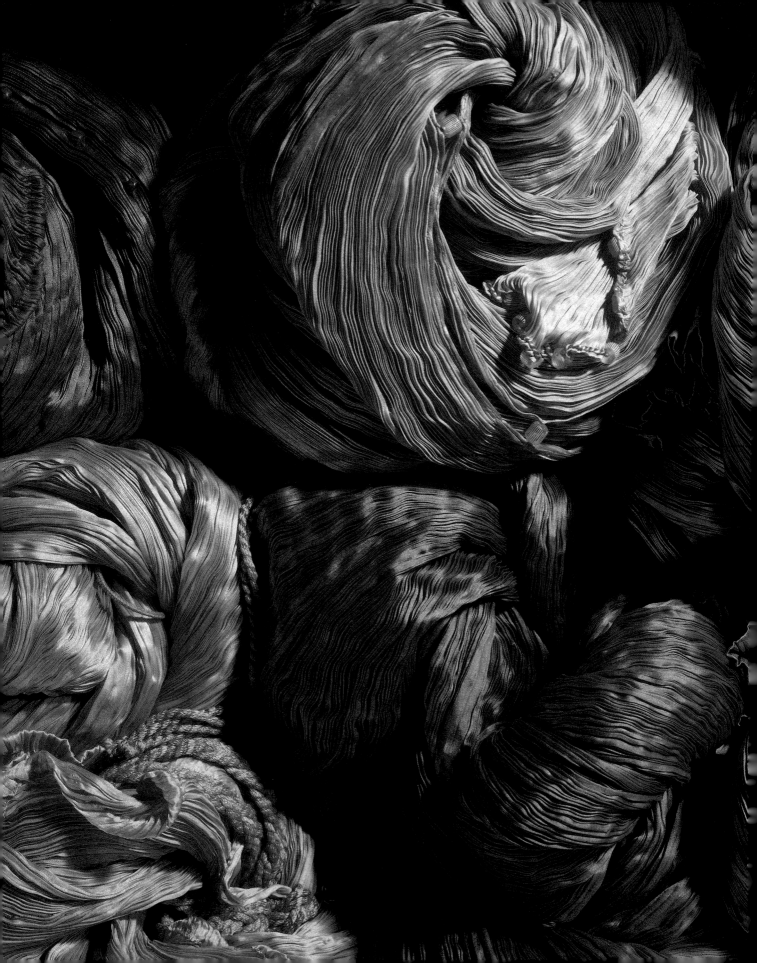

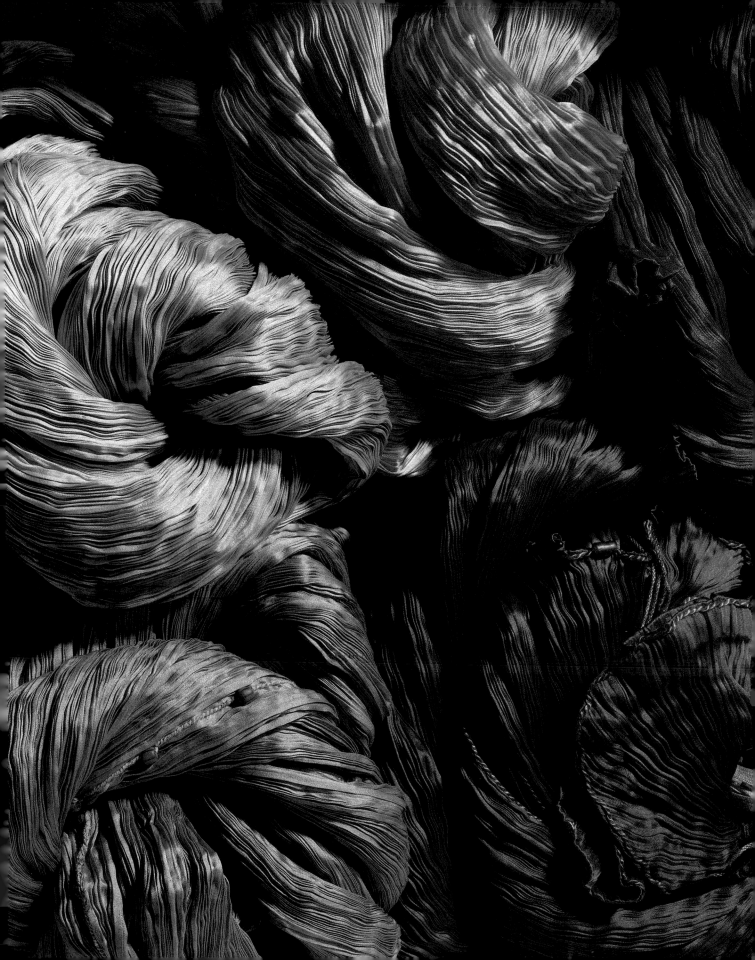

INTIMATE ICONOGRAPHY

————

Art's Witness to Dressing

We enter the boudoir of the other through the optic of art. Painting provides access beyond the public world of display into a more personal sphere of discretion. Painting intrudes, often with some politesse though occasionally with none, into the act of dressing. Art celebrates the rituals of apparel and appearance-making. The visual arts distinguish dress and undress and all the layers in between.

Art confronts us with the body. More abruptly, art confronts us with clothing. Modern art encounters nudity, the disrobed, and the dressed with an equanimity that fostered the myth of the avant-garde. Édouard Manet's *Déjeuner sur l'Herbe* (1863) presents male figures in full dress with female figures disrobed. The affront that Manet sought was, of course, achieved when some spectators found the painting and its imputed circumstance scandalous. But art had long been disclosing the very process of dressing, lingering over the stages of bareness and covering, luxuriating in a witness permitted to the painter's eye but otherwise often shaded by culture's soft light from the risks of lust and luxury. Manet's bold gesture was only to give dramatic contrast to what art had been observing with some lust, but with the excuse of vigilance.

In the eighteenth century, dressing was a ceremony in and of itself. The royal levee was a ritual of importance in that it represented royalty in the first phase of day and dress. Secular and courtly time was gauged with the same deliberation as the religious hours, a grand clock of propriety and daily activity. Rigorous adherence to the schedule of apparel was required to achieve the activities of the day. All protocols emanate from, or at least correspond to, appropriate clothing. J.-F. de Troy's *The Declaration of Love* (1724) reveals

Page 29: Pablo Picasso, *Girl in a Chemise,* 1905

itself in clothing as in narrative. The loosened laces of the lady's gown indicate the intimacy of the occasion.

How does one come to the exchange of affectionate thoughts in the grand setting of this interior, but by the informal deportment and casual attire? Twentieth-century views and versions of the eighteenth century, especially in film, have tended to bifurcate a frigid Court style and libidinous *jeux d'amour* with décolletage. A much more subtle social spectrum prevailed in the Age of Enlightenment, clothing calibrating day and night and specifying the levels of discourse formal and informal. The unfastened bodice is neither libido nor license alone, but is a style of casual interaction. Thus, the painting is a declaration of love in the quiet room and the personal exchange where art has the capability of bearing silent, attentive witness. Court dressing was, of course, an attended activity, one that could not be performed alone, but that required servants. Intrinsically, dressing was with witness.

Art and cultural criticism today has conditioned us to see sexuality and gender as primary terms of representation. Dress, thereby, is symptomatic but not significant. Perhaps, though, these matters so critical to our time were secondary in some ways to the issue of dress in an earlier time. That is, dress may have been the foremost index to such secondary matters as level of personal exchange and the behavioral zones of public and private. In this conjecture, a painting such as Manet's *Déjeuner sur l'Herbe* is less surprising: its antipodal dress vs. undress is only the extreme version of our indicative role of dress in assessing eighteenth- and nineteenth-century painting.

Portraiture, in such context, is sensitive to dress not only as the artifact most directly involving the subject but also as the key to the desired interaction—formal or informal—between the subject and spectator. When Élisabeth Vigée-Lebrun showed Marie Antoinette in the muslin *chemise à la reine*, the pretext was in part the bucolic setting of the Petit Trianon, the flower plucked, and the straw hat, but the relative change in dress from the formal satin gowns in which the queen had formerly been depicted was startling. The softened, reduced manner of dress is similarly represented in David's

Page 31: Jacques-Louis David, *Antoine Laurent Lavoisier and His Wife,* 1788

portrait titled *Antoine Laurent Lavoisier and His Wife* (1788), in which the new style worn by the scientist's wife makes her seem especially muse-like and diaphanous. Her clothing, so newly brought from boudoir intimacy into the light of day, is as emblematic of the rationalist's impulse to scrutiny as the scientific equipment on Monsieur Lavoisier's table. The elegance of F. X. Winterhalter's Second Empire tableaux and portraits derives from his artistic penchant for the soft dress of the period that was almost as much lingerie as it was external dress and thereby constitutes a bridge between intimate and external apparel.

But men, too, enjoyed a portraiture at relaxation. They were depicted at ease wearing the banyan in an eighteenth-century style, as in John Singleton Copley's portrait *Joseph Sherburne* (ca. 1767–70). The dressing gown, though a garment exclusively for the home, was as sumptuous and resplendent as any clothing worn more publicly. Generations later, the same garment remains one of the most decorated options in an elegant man's wardrobe, its visual tradition perhaps accounting in part for its persistence. If one considers that the dressing gown and its counterpart in the *robe volante* were visible only in privileged intimacy, their principal spectatorship comes from paintings. Similarly, women might be caught in the moments between undress and dress, sometimes in the dressing gown. Manet's *Woman with a Parrot* wore such a gown in the mid-1860s, at a time when the staging of dress once associated chiefly with the Court passed to the bourgeoisie. Manet's puckish provocation acknowledges the tradition of witnessed dressing and also its increasing indelicacy in the nineteenth century. Of course, a century later, Yves Saint Laurent realizes the Manet painting as a source for a re-created dressing gown intended to be worn as evening wear. Significantly, the Saint Laurent gown still conveys the sense of the dressing gown that is its origin. It is transformed, but its source is not denied.

Manet, of course, tenders actual lingerie and *maquillage* in his painting *Nana* (1877), which identifies the nineteenth-century awareness of intimate apparel. During the same

Page 32: J.-F. de Troy, *The Declaration of Love,* 1724

Page 34: John Singleton Copley, *Joseph Sherburne,* ca. 1767–70

Page 35: European, *Man's banyan,* ca. 1780

decades in which dress was externalizing the elements of intimate apparel and intimate apparel was emulating the decoration of clothing concomitantly and even more ardently, art was entering the private world of dress like the ubiquitous top-hatted gentleman/voyeur. Even if we resent the intrusion of the mustachioed observer so close to Nana, he is the modern spectator who lacks reticence, seeing clothing in layers of textile, time, and confidentiality. As Nana cocks her head in the viewer's direction, we share clothing secrets no longer concealed at all. Georges Seurat's *Jeune femme se poudrant* (1888–90) is perhaps as narcissistically involved in the cosmetic act, but our attentiveness is the inevitable accompaniment and justification of this act of beauty-making in the midst of an observed process of dressing.

Narrative is likewise imputed to dressing in nineteenth-century art, often in stories that capture women in the gaze and under the command of men. In William Holman Hunt's *The Awakening Conscience* (1853) and Degas's *Interior* (also called *The Rape*) (1868–69), female dress is used to deal with the issues of vulnerability and exploitation.

Apart from these coerced entries into the boudoir, intimate apparel has been gladly brought into view precisely as its ambiguity with apparent dress has been manifest in the nineteenth and twentieth centuries. Thus, the F. X. Winterhalter *Elizabeth, Empress of Austria* (1864) seems to stand as fountainhead to the suite of Pre-Raphaelite images of women in aesthetic dress, sensible apparel, and casual appearance. The foreground figure in Raimundo de Madrazo y Garreta's *Girls at a Window* is on the borderline between private space and the collective view in her peignoir, in contrast to her background companion who is fully dressed. From portraits that drew monarchy to a close and established the classical and reductive sensibility of the modern to a sympathetic 1905 painting by Pablo Picasso of a *Girl in a Chemise*, there is a shared sense of the probity of simple attire, that which began as undergarment, serving as art's sign of dress and art's seduction that permits us to realize an idea as complicated as dress through a metaphor as simple as a chemise. Little surprise, of course, is there that Karl Lagerfeld for Chanel and Carmelo Pomodoro create ribbed undershirts that go from the most rudimentary

Page 37: Raimundo de Madrazo y Garreta, *Girls at a Window*, n.d.

form of dress to the most sophisticated. Each, of course, enjoys as well the differentiation between the commonplace underwear-derived tank top and a more conventionally elegant skirt, to say nothing of the fact that this men's undergarment has been usurped by women.

Art did not invent the dressing process, though that process is clearly a cultural artifice. But art has made us acutely aware of dress as symbol and of the workings of apparel as a means of claiming beauty.

Page 39: Édouard Manet, *Woman with a Parrot* (detail), n.d.

Page 41: Yves Saint Laurent
for Christian Dior,
Evening dress,
spring/summer 1960

Page 42: Karl Lagerfeld
for Chanel,
Evening ensemble, 1992

Page 43: *Marky Mark
(Mark Wahlberg),* 1993.
Photograph Herb Ritts
for Calvin Klein

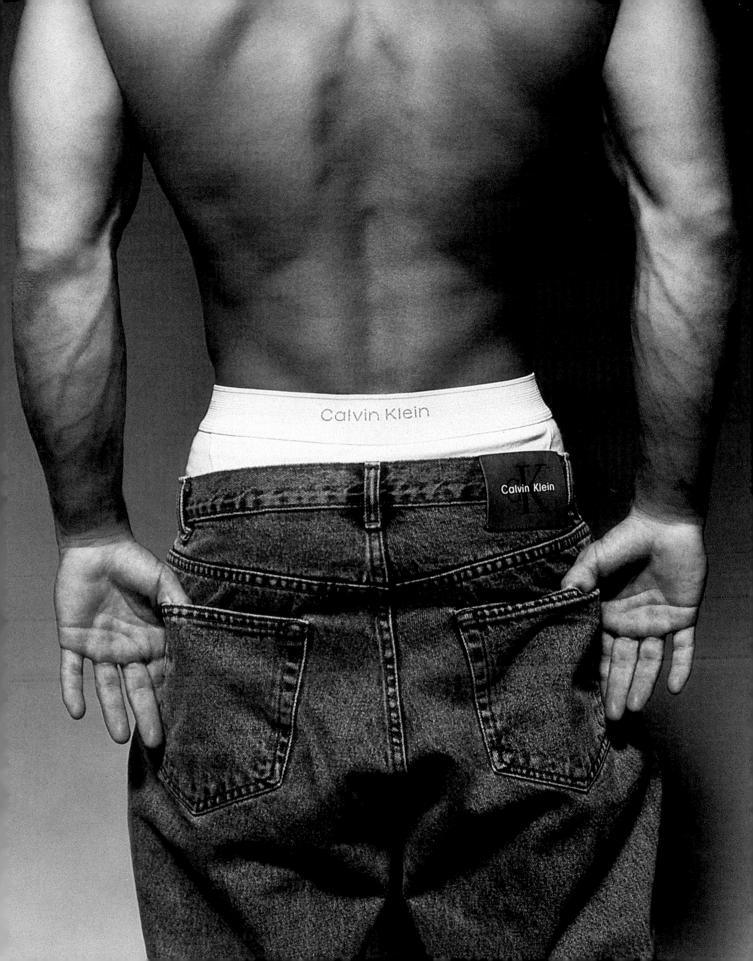

ARCHITECTONIC EXPERIENCE

The Corset and Body Shape

We fashion our body shape. Whether it is eighteenth-century dress, the New Look, or contemporary style, the most important configuration of appearance is the determination of silhouette, a self-conscious resolution that the body will be represented in proportions and measure decided or desired as a standard of beauty.

Contemporary fashion is fascinated by body shaping and the corset. That fascination can be justified historically in the manner offered by David Kunzle in the 1982 volume *Fashion and Fetishism: A Social History of the Corset, Tight-Lacing and Other Forms of Body-Sculpture in the West*, in which Kunzle concludes, "The capacity to transmute that physical pain [constriction] into pleasure is a mystery that neither physiology nor psychology may ever solve.... It is tied to certain unique historical moments in the struggle for social and sexual liberation, a struggle that will never again manifest itself in quite the same form, but which nevertheless continues." Recent works by Jean Paul Gaultier, Karl Lagerfeld for Fendi, and Gianni Versace, among others, demonstrate the endless desire to explore such shape-giving structures even as they may be acknowledged as anachronistic. Even in an era when we know the cultural cast of a woman's body to be one of the last and most personal imprisonments of the doll's house, the dress object and body objectification still conspire—at least on occasion—to define body shape as sculpture. Indisputably, but often with argument that is hyperbolic or specious, body shaping is related to cultural perceptions of the erogenous. Yet, the corset's revival in recent fashion may be as much about historicism and internal awareness in dress as it is about erogeny per se.

Page 45: Édouard Manet, *Nana,* 1877

A 1991 corset bathing suit by Fendi, for example, reembodies the historical form of the corset, though much of the structure is now easily supplanted by Lycra, as it also is in other contemporary swimwear. The anachronism of the garment is paramount, even as it is subverted from a garment of subjugation to beauty into a prerogative of historical reclamation. The Fendi bathing suit is sufficiently referential to the corset that no swimmer would elect to wear it without knowing its sources; the cognitive and deeply affective association with the historical exemplar of the corset seems to be reversed into the relatively liberated, physically free activity of swimming and modern swimwear. At the same time, the Fendi swimsuit makes apparent the transformation from an inner layer to the peel: what had been internal to dress comes self-consciously to the surface. Does the subversive change of the garment declare that the corset is now only to be mocked, or does it retrieve the possibility of the corset in some degree of oppression? Fashion designers with a vivid sense of the history of costume, such as Gaultier, Lacroix, and Versace, have employed the corset with witty delight in its aberrational, anachronistic presence in a contemporary wardrobe. Irony and clever intelligence are the operative modes under which the corset has been reinstated. Saint Laurent's structural renewal is of the Belle Époque, while Valentino revives the "New Look" merry widow.

The corset cleaves and cinches the waist, by impression or by physical impress, then enhancing the bosom as it is lifted up by the corset constriction. Shaping was created through bone, busk, and stays to form an artificial rib embracing the body more tightly than nature's willingness to contract. The corset was laced tightly on all public occasions in the eighteenth century, but it was once again a sign of intimacy among women: when alone, they could loosen the laces and establish a more informal atmosphere.

Costume history records the great periods of anatomical constriction. During the nineteenth century, a severely shaped human geometry prevailed. After a relatively brief period in the early part of the twentieth century, during which the corset was more or less abandoned, the calipers of shaping returned in the 1940s and 1950s with the New Look. With the prevailing return of shape, Jacques Fath pursued the logical reversion to

Page 46: Georges Seurat, *Jeune fille se poudrant,* 1888–90

primary cause, simulating the corset as an evening dress bodice, tied with tight lacing. Does Fath thereby betray the New Look in making us realize that it is not so new after all but is instead the revival of the hourglass shaping effected through corsetry? In the disclosure of the internal structure, there is also the confession to historical affinities and sources that gives the Fath dress unashamed audacity.

Does the Toulouse-Lautrec voyeur or any kindred fetishist of tight lacing inevitably reappear with the style? Like any historical revival, the corset carries with it cultural implications and collective memories. Even more vividly, erotic memory may never fade, but the late twentieth-century uses of the corset are acutely self-aware, decisively clothing-bonded design concepts that have uncertain connection to the customarily connected issues of gender, fetishism, and physical/psychological oppression and gratification. Kunzle cites the representational traditions associated with the corset, including the *essai du corset* (corset fitting), a frequently epochal struggle between the staymaker and his pulling and the seeming victim's body.

That we see the corset flitting back and forth in history is one observation, but we are also aware that the corset oscillates between public and private view. The corset or its semblance was visible on the surface in the eighteenth century. In its revived form in the period from 1810 to 1860, it was seldom ostensible, though its shaping effects are apparent. The "secret" of post-War couture is no private matter to Fath. In regional dress, the decorated, embroidered, and embellished corset is frequently an element of external dress, worn over the chemise and shirt. The corset epitomizes infra-structure's flickering relationship between the visible and the invisible. Like an architectural element that under one sensibility appears and in another disappears, it is nonetheless a building component, a way of constructing even when it is unseen.

Bernard Rudofsky's concept of the "unfashionable human body" is that shape was made to conform to social standards of beauty and utility. The body, after all, can accommodate some shaping: inevitably, it is the given armature for clothing and a limit to clothing's invention.

Page 49: Henri de Toulouse-Lautrec, *Femme à sa toilette,* 1896

Page 51: *Madonna,* 1990,
wearing Jean Paul Gaultier,
"Like a Virgin" corset, 1990.
Photograph by
Jean-Baptiste Mondino

Page 52: Gianni Versace,
Corset gown,
fall/winter 1991–92

Page 53: Gianni Versace,
left: *Slip dress,*
fall/winter 1991–92;
right: *Baby doll dress,*
fall/winter 1991–92

Page 55: Yves Saint Laurent,
left: *Corset dress,*
fall/winter 1991–92;
right: *Corset dress,*
fall/winter 1991–92

Page 56: Thierry Mugler,
Corset suit,
fall/winter 1992–93

Page 57: Belville Sassoon,
Evening bodice, ca. 1985,
shown with Perry Ellis skirt

Page 58: Jacques Fath,
Evening gown, 1947

Page 59: Jacques Fath,
Evening gown (detail), 1947

Page 60: Valentino [Garavani],
Evening gown,
fall/winter 1992–93

Page 61: Jean Paul Gaultier,
Evening dress, 1992

SECRET STRATEGIES

The Vocabulary of Undress

Lingerie seduced clothing in the nineteenth century. Within a few decades of its impertinent disclosure, lingerie retreated in the 1820s to the private realm, retaining its relatively functional simplicity even as the gowns it influenced developed increasingly complex surfaces. Throughout the nineteenth century, lingerie inspired by the decorative vocabulary of white gowns, developed in a manner akin to the architecture of the period until lingerie became, itself, a great patternbook of apparel decoration. The cache of intimate apparel from immediate view allowed the evolution of a style both hermetic and rich, a private profligacy developed to excess in the modest reserve from public scrutiny. By century's end, all apparel was enjoying the techniques originated in elaborate toilettes preserved and perfected in intimate apparel. Undergarments became the envy of their layered neighbors. By 1900, apparel was emulating undergarments, because they were the most extravagant forms of dress, employing the most sophisticated and highly evolved techniques and delights in clothing. Hidden from view, elaboration and decoration flourished until they were more than undergarments could bear and they themselves were bared.

The greenhouse-forced cultivation of the decorative was stratified by the design demands of the decades, following the large developments of nineteenth-century taste through historical revivals and spirited renewals of interests in technique. Scroll and foliate motives were the first to appear on the initially plain undergarments; the romantic revival added Elizabethan slashings, puffed sleeves, decorated bodices, sleeve caps, and hems. Subsequently, shirred bands, panels of broderie anglaise, insets of Valenciennes

Page 63: F. X. Winterhalter, *Mme Rimsky-Korsakov*, 1864

lace, point d'esprit, silk ribbons, and pintucking constituted a highly expansive, almost colonial, grammar of ornament, responsive to stylistic interests in domesticity and dress. Like Steven Marcus's "other" in the Victorian era, intimate apparel was prodigally sensuous and ornamentally indulgent. Dress reformers advocated wool undergarments and practicality in intimate apparel in the 1880s and 1890s precisely because the sensibility of the time enjoyed the gloss of silk and muslin and handkerchief linen elaborated in rosettes, lace, ribbon, and embroidery as an undeniable but clandestine vice of indulgence.

Decoration especially prospered as undergarments became more and more voluminous, creating the shapes of nineteenth-century dress. "Fictitious curves," as C.W. and Phillis Cunnington describe in *The History of Underclothes* of nineteenth-century intimate apparel, were not confined to shaping of the bust and waist; they also induced the creation of great arcs and hoops of soft, billowing form that expanded upon the volume of the body from the waist down. Amplitude was achieved in a manner far different from the volume of eighteenth-century dress: hoops and cages might define form, but the body's extension, even up to the bustles of the end of the century, was accomplished in petticoats and other soft forms. Fashion historian Elizabeth Ewing expressed her amazement at late nineteenth-century underpinnings:"There was no end to the elaborations of the petticoats of the last twenty years of the nineteenth century. A pink satin petticoat of the 1880s is more than four yards wide at the hem, above which it is lined and stiffened. Deep folds at the back draw the fullness there. All but the main seams are hand-sewn, including all the frills." Clothing was beginning to be industrialized, and Singer's invention of the sewing machine was to transform the nature of clothing. But undergarments were the most obdurately ornamented and fastidiously handmade of fashion garments, insisting upon their special status close to the body, preserving privacy and finesse in an increasingly public world. Even the elements of shaping came to be embellished and thereafter emulated in dress. Corsets were externalized in the girdle of Venus or the Gobelin corselet, the latter a belt in the mid-1860s that defined bust and waistline but was trimmed in the back with a visible ruffle of lace.

Of course, Victorian dilation of shape and delectation in underwear decoration only added to the mystique of the undergarment. A lingerie dress, a filmy cumulus in silk or finessed lawn, appropriated the fine arts of lingerie to give some public testimony to the qualities of apparel creation. Demimondaines gave much credence to the bourgeois taste for embellished undergarments, serving as a vanguard that brought morning dresses, tea gowns, and wrappers into a wider world of view. But it was not long before high style followed the demimonde in delighting in a peek at the demi-toilette.

Semi-public articles of clothing enjoyed extended use, as they were among the most beautiful, delicate, and expensive items in the trousseaux and wardrobes of elegant women. Combing ensembles, morning dresses, Watteau wrappers, and dressing gowns were coming to the fore late in the nineteenth century as underwear had a century before; they were now the custom of the day for the new bourgeoisie. Even in the twentieth century, the self-conscious creation of dress from the elements of lingerie by designers such as Chanel and Vionnet emphasizes the luxury and special handmade qualities of intimate apparel.

Innermost layers of clothing held the utmost appeal and truest sign of quality. Even as the undergarment was the inevitable trope to eroticism, it equally signified handmade clothing, ornamentation in abundance with good taste, and luxury in material. Thus, in the early years of the twentieth century, the sheer slip dresses of Boué Soeurs and the Callots brought to the dress the valued properties of lingerie. A sweetness of artisanal performance was married to an ideal of simplicity in Boué Soeurs. The Callots mixed harem-like veilings in hot oriental colors and fragile metallic laces in chemises of languorous eroticism. A Chanel dress in soft layers of lingerie transparency and finishing is created in the paradigm of lingerie but for evening wear. In the twentieth century, the processes of lingerie, including faggoting, picot finishing, and pinked edges, are increasingly brought to external dress, as if to simulate underclothing and give to modern clothing the anachronism and intimacy of underclothes. At the same time, the softened silhouettes of the 1920s and 1930s depended upon the techniques of soft construction as they had been perfected in intimate apparel. The pragmatic American designer Claire McCardell chose to create evening classicism out of the materials associated with sleep-wear and lingerie. Sonia Rykiel, Issey Miyake, and others have seized the techniques of lingerie finishing as self-conscious applications to daywear, there to stand as intimate signifiers.

Page 67:
F. X. Winterhalter,
*Elizabeth, Empress
of Austria,* 1864

Pages 68–69:
F. X. Winterhalter,
*Empress Eugénie and
Her Ladies of Honor,* 1855

Page 70: French,
Wedding dress, 1864

Page 71: American,
*Corset covers
and combing jackets,*
late nineteenth century

Page 72: American,
Petticoats, 1880–1907

Page 73: American,
Reception dress, late 1870s

Page 75: American,
Lingerie dress, ca. 1877

Page 76: European,
Dress (detail), ca. 1818

Page 77: American,
Dress, early 1840s

Page 79: left: English,
Day dress, ca. 1833–34;
right: American,
Day dress, ca. 1842

Pages 80–81: American,
Dress (detail), 1840s

Page 83: French,
Wedding dress
(detail), ca. 1837

Page 84: left: American,
Semi-evening dress,
ca. 1903–4;
right: American,
Afternoon dress, ca. 1908

Page 85: American,
Semi-evening dress
(detail), ca. 1903–4

Page 86: Boué Soeurs,
Robe de style, ca. 1920

Page 87: Boué Soeurs,
Robe de style
(detail), ca. 1920

Page 89: Lucile,
left: *Dress,* ca. 1912;
right: *Tea dance dress,*
ca. 1916–17

Pages 90–91: Lucile,
Tea dance dress (detail),
ca. 1916–17

Page 92: Bill Blass,
Evening dress, ca. 1987

Page 93: Bergdorf Goodman,
*Evening dress and
jacket,* 1938

ANALYTICAL APPAREL

Deconstruction and Discovery in Contemporary Costume

The modernist W. B. Yeats thought the center would not hold. Ironically, the center holds fast; all that surrounds it is in dispersal.

The thesis that fashion has tended to examine and expose its elements and armature flows into another corpus of knowledge and body awareness in the twentieth century, most especially late in the century. If the structure of clothing is a continuous cultural cognition and recurring manifestation, recent dress has, in a suite of compelling instances, associated with forward fashion, torn clothing asunder as if to reveal thereby, in the most impassioned and importuned manner, elements of clothing exposed. One realizes the shimmering beauty of a Fendi fur coat that is seemingly destroyed to become evocatively and aesthetically richer than conventional furs. In an era of T-shirt dressing, Marc Jacobs for Perry Ellis destroys the T-shirt in order to reconstitute its vision. In two great campaigns at the beginning of the 1980s and 1990s, Rei Kawakubo for Comme des Garçons has made a clothing ab ovo, exposing structure but more apparently suggesting ravages. Late in the twentieth century, popular culture has repeatedly slashed, spoiled, and distressed clothing to render it of refurbished vitality. High fashion has worked more analytically to offer a prolonged interest in apparel: destruction becomes a process of analytical creation.

The intellectual model for such fashion practice is deconstruction. Deconstruction insists that we take what exists as a coherent whole and discern constituent parts that are in themselves oppositional. But even that tough-minded regimen of the mind has its visual romantic counterpart in the enchantment with ruins, the long tradition of enjoying

Page 95: Comme des Garçons, *Day ensembles,* 1981, Photograph by Peter Lindbergh for Comme des Garçons, 1983

the remnants for their evocation of what had existed previously. Clothing conforms to this Ozymandias vision and even creates new forms that are aged artificially or perturbed in appearance to suggest the wrecked and ravaged. Of course, a popular-culture counterpart is recycling, the concept that worthy constituents of one creation become elements for a subsequent generation, though structure may change and cultural chaff will be blown away.

For clothing, the creative counterpart of deconstruction as a theoretical discipline is found in the work of Karl Lagerfeld. Lagerfeld's evident regard for clothing as manufacture was given elegant witness in his final collection for his first years at Chloe, in which he incorporated the motives of seamstresses and of apparel making into the clothing. His second phase of design leadership at Chloe in 1992–93 is already marked by a transparency of clothing layers and an almost flower-like revelation of costume layers and structure. Similarly, Lagerfeld for Chanel has exposed not only the most conventional—but anomalous for the couture—underwear briefs in 1993, but also the taxonomy of Chanel motifs, deliberately and extravagantly presented as the historian's attestation and the aficionado's intemperance. For Fendi, Lagerfeld has reversed and exposed and stripped, bringing clothing's secrets to the surfaces and allowing the luxury beneath the finest creation of clothing to be apparent. Lagerfeld exemplifies the connoisseur's intelligence about clothing. He delves into the interior and intensity of a garment to realize its power and to realize what it is physically, bringing those to the unavoidable witness of the spectator.

In the context of Infra-Apparel, deconstruction may seem to be the reasoning *avant la lettre*. Is there an inherent difference, let us say, between Vionnet's radical exposure of the garment's techniques and the deconstruction of Lagerfeld and Kawakubo? Making and breaking are, in this sense, a continuity, but the presupposition of the late-twentieth-century examples seems to be that they are working back from a finished garment, ravaging its integrity rather than showing the process of making. Arguably, the emotional stakes are raised somewhere in the ambiguous zone between the positive values of making and the treacherous values of destroying. The roses that gather shape and yet seem unfinished in a Vionnet dress are the imperfect, being/becoming flowers of no corsage but of some interstice between the flower in formation and in decay. Our poignant equivocation with respect to the Vionnet roses anticipates many of the ideas about elements of composing and decomposing evident in late-twentieth-century clothing.

In fact, there is a story, an insinuation of topic and even narrative, frequently allied with the presence of deconstruction in contemporary costume. In a 1985 essay "Rei Kawakubo and the Aesthetic of Poverty," one of the present authors, Harold Koda, argues for an apolitical, zen philosophical reading of the early-1980s knotted, apparently disheveled, and "lace" (i.e., with holes) garments of Comme des Garçons. A decade after Kawakubo's seminal work—admittedly foreshadowed to some degree by the obstreperous, overly political punk styles of Vivienne Westwood—we have returned to images of poverty, premises of despoilment, a mystique of the ruin and decay, and a proclivity to the analysis of form in its defiled form, not in its innocence. Indeed, as Koda pointed out, our difficulty in analyzing such fashion lies in our Western prejudices regarding the creative process and our assumption that all ideas originate in purity. A century ago, the 1890s saw decadence as an aesthetic ideal. In another way and yet one that reveals us to cleave to century's close and millennium's imminence, fashion in the 1990s is looking to models of decomposition and decay as sources of creativity.

Worldwide recession in the 1990s has had a profound cultural impact, not least on fashion. Koda's dialectic of the "poor look" with America's affluent "financially optimistic, conspicuous consumers" already seems optimistic. Any observer would note the tendency in American fashion to play down wealth and promote the democracy of clothing preferences, not to fulfill de Tocqueville but for simple economic reasons. A chastened wardrobe of the late twentieth century is in formation. In straitened economic circumstances, perhaps we look at the poor and symbols of poverty differently. High-style impoverishment is evident in the 1990s and coincides as the narrative and picturesque sibling of physical destruction and deconstruction.

Global recession is more than academic or economic theory. It can quicken every person to realize that he or she may be on the economic wheel of fortune, a candidate for misfortune. At least in the large journalistic descriptives, one would not have imagined that the affluent customers of Bloomingdale's thought their positions were easily reversed with beggars and bag ladies of the period. Of course, empathy and compassion should always exist: sometimes the force majeure is circumstance. Sustained economic decline, a new expectation of diminished standards of living, and substantive white-collar unemployment compel compassion and promote proximity, not the Darwinism and distance of the 1980s. In the 1990s, we feel the fragility of economic status and tend to avoid its flamboyance.

If we could have imagined that we were at a cool philosophical distance from poverty or in a position to make a political statement by wearing oversized, tangled, and monochromatic clothing a decade ago, that position has been preempted by popular fashion in its spectrum of A/X denim-and-worker predilection, fastidious blue-collar-meets-the-Main-Line of the Gap and Banana Republic, and even the street-smart slouch of Girbaud, Levi's Loose, and Cross Colours. In the 1990s, even Armani tailored clothing for men has sacrificed its power-suit authority to become something close to Chaplinesque tenderness in silhouette along with suitably softened sentiment.

But prole penchants, however symptomatic they may be, are nonetheless still separate from discrete references to impoverishment and homelessness. In fact, Kawakubo's references in 1991 and 1992 are as veiled, as it were, as her references were in the 1980s. Her new poor look is a rich imagery of deconstruction, romantic decay, and analytical disclosure of structure. If her garments seem to have moldered with the wedding dress of Dickens' Miss Havisham, the Kawakubo clothing endures to be worn even in its impoverished and importuned state. Tattered edges, evacuated sections, and mismatched mate-

Page 99: Comme des Garçons, *Lace sweater*, fall/winter 1982–83.
Photograph by Peter Lindbergh for Comme des Garçons, 1982

rials may be anathema to a middle-class value in the same way in which Chanel appropriated jersey and the little black dress from the working class. Chanel's class-conscious boule-versement would, of course, have lasting impact and the middle class would have to accept once-reviled materials and a once-rejected style as fundamental options for mod-ern fashion design. Social equity can be achieved in transformations of clothing types. Are we able to distinguish rich and poor in terms of clothing? The common-sense answer is, of course, that we can or that we would think we can. Perhaps it is in the very circumstance of thinking clothing distinguishes between rich and poor that it becomes effective in its instances of mediation and transgression: rich becoming poor and poor seeming to be rich. Thorstein Veblen thought, of course, that he had a classic and immu-table example of conspicuous consumption in apparel. The history of sumptuary laws would suggest the veracity of Veblen's assumption that clothing would invariably be economically coded. In the instance of deconstructed clothing, however, we can watch the fascinating case in our time of clothing defying the conventional codes and providing a paradox of style and conscience remarkably fit, as it were, for our time of dramatic economic reordering. To be sure, any high style may offer a kind of *nostalgie de la boue*. Fashion photography has often imperiled fine apparel by surprising circumstance or context. For example, Richard Avedon's famous 1955 *Harper's Bazaar* photograph "Dovima with Elephants," photographed at the Cirque D'Hiver, gains its tension and frisson in large part from the fragility of the model and the dress poised a little too perilously between frisky pachyderms. But not even Avedon expected the conventional wearer of Dior to prance with the elephants. Paul Gallico's *Mrs. 'Arris Goes to Paris* reminds us that a British charwoman could be so smitten by a Dior gown that she would ultimately merit it by social and moral traversal. Cinderella likewise tended a hearth until the significant dress and shoes served to transform her into a beauty fit for a prince's gaze. Perhaps clothing maintains its symbolic value because we believe such tales of clothing's eleva-tion of the wearer to extraordinary stature. If we so believe, perhaps we also posit that the suburbanite wearing workers' clothes via Ralph Lauren is likewise transfigured in an opposite direction to become Rosie the Riveter or a Thomas Hart Benton hero of the land placed into a Scarsdale backyard.

That Kawakubo's poor look of 1982–83 looks unsurprising to us today is not only because its avant-garde incredulity has dissipated, but also because, once again, we have accommodated so much of what was once avant-garde to our conventional styles. Kawakubo's clothing remains as resolutely philosophical and meditative as Koda argued of it in the1980s, but we are more and more thinking alike. Deconstruction in clothing is an idea made evident in clothing's proclivity to manifest itself, is burnished in today's intellectual concetti of clothing, and is topical in its large and engaging cultural issues. Karl Lagerfeld, Issey Miyake, Marithe and François Girbaud, and other designers have been pioneers of deconstructed clothing through the 1980s, but the watershed of thinking and praxis has occurred only at the beginning of the 1990s.

In fall–winter 1991, Christian Francis Roth paired two epic and vestigial American themes in his collection: quilts and hoboes. The high-style hobo suits that Roth created are no cold-beans-out-of-the-can variety. Undisguised, vivid patches—consummate examples of the exquisite Roth artistry of piecing—inflect the wool color fields as delicate compositions in color. The patches as used by Roth are so conspicuous that they become badges of pride, visible elements of poverty. We do not mistake the Roth for true poverty any more than we think the Kawakubo desuetude is authentic or the Fendi coat is genuinely in disarray. Rather, we come to terms with it in an indirect, picturesque way. Our ideal of the train-hopping, itinerant, but never menacing, vagrant helped out at the back door of houses in small towns is a piece of American nostalgia akin to Hope, Arkansas. To be sure, these vanished and/or vanishing places and values assume mythic importance late in the century as we lose them. Today, drugs and other circumstances have made the homeless population seemingly more volatile, lethal, and frightening than the benign hobo. The child of the 1920s and 1930s saw the hobo with wanderlust valor. Freddy the

Freeloader and the Little Tramp were vagabond heroes long before post-war culture made the image of wanderers wild ones. Patches were common-sense Americana, yielding increased utility to a garment. Despite some hippie revival in the late 1960s and early 1970s, patches have all but vanished from the American scene, even in hard times. Roth was creating an epic figure and was using as a design element something that was patently vestigial and nostalgic. If Kawakubo delights in atavism and Lagerfeld in intellectual luxe, Roth cherishes remembrance and yearning, even beyond the outstanding quality of his work. One of the reasons Roth is most successful as a designer is that he has a sentimental spirit that gives soul and sensation to every garment. His 1992 trompe l'oeil corset dress gives a storytelling directness to the permeable layers of clothing that other designers see in shredding and exposing.

Poverty had dignity. Then. It is that "then" to which we are taken in Kawakubo's scholastic sensibility and in Roth's recollective longing. So, too, Yukio Kobayashi's misscaled, mismatched patches and tatters in Matsuda menswear for fall–winter 1992 convey yearning. More pensive, perhaps, than Roth, Kobayashi takes us only to the genteel dandy who has long served as *typos* for Kobayashi's vision of the modern man. The shabby dandy (only apparently shabby, of course) is likewise effective in Matsuda menswear, always superb in execution, for its evocative power. In the same season, Paul Smith, Andrew Fezza, and Dolce e Gabbana have similarly offered a clochard to Beau Brummel synthesis in the appearance of patches, abraded sections, and vacated elements. We seem to have entered Charles Ryder's world, and each apparel malapropism or rip is only sophomoric disdain or exceptional gentility nonchalantly snagged on every protruding nail of the manor.

In the 1930s, Carl Becker, the great historian, wrote, "Economic distress will teach men, if anything can, that realities are less dangerous than fancies, that fact-finding is more effective than fault-finding." The default that has marked the world economy in the 1990s has had remarkable consequences for fashion. Among those consequences is fashion's desire to portray poverty. Arguably, fashion in these late years of the twentieth

Page 103: Martin Margiela, *"Lining" dress,* 1991. Photograph by Martin Margiela

century has become as chastened as Becker suggested that it might be under economic constraint. "Fancies" have been forsaken in hard times, yet no metaphor can ever be lost and no dream denied. An imagery of poverty, a recognition of social ills, can yield a *Grapes of Wrath* as readily, if not more so, as it constricts the human spirit. Fashion designers in the 1990s may not be exacting social justice, but they are realizing the ceaseless role of imagination in and upon the economic order. Fashion can still make a prince or a princess into a pauper and vice versa. In that aptitude, there is unbounded richness and there is inventive hope for all. If Tara's drapes could become the post-bellum ball gown, fashion renewed the Cinderella dream. One realizes there is a vision in realizing the deconstruction—the dynamic of fashion making and fashion destroying—of contemporary dress. Such clothing is the ruin in the landscape, a picaresque of past and promise of the future.

The skeleton of a structure by Martin Margiela, seemingly partial and patched, is a violation only of our expectation of clothing's unbroken entity. The completeness and coherence of such a garment is made more evident by its breach, void, and bond, each element calling our attention to clothing's composition. Like a poetic language that in a combination of concinnity and complexity is at variance with our day-to-day speech, such poetic dress only affirms our desire to speak and our need to communicate, in this instance, of clothing. Even in the instance of Comme des Garçons, the collections of 1992 and 1993 are less referential to poverty and abandonment and are instead more analytical and rigorously reasoned as clothing construction.

Is our contemporary conclusion to an an argument of clothing's open discourse with its own structure and inner workings more foreboding and sinister than we would have hoped from the whitework conversation of the nineteenth century (lingerie informing dress and vice versa) or from the culturally genteel entry to boudoirs and women's private circles? To some, it may seem an apocalyptic and nightmarish ending to a fancy fantasy. But no such dire conclusion is necessary if we perceive the historical role of dress. Constant in addressing issues of the private and the disclosed, apparel is a phenomenon of personal and cultural interaction. Deconstruction, a model of thought current to our time, provides a metaphor for the capacity of clothing to migrate between the personal and public spheres. Dress arouses innate feelings of individual expression and intimacy; dress determines the nature of social exchange among individuals. The direct observation of clothing's fervent claim to the public intellect is only the current form of clothing's constant demand to analyze itself and us.

Page 115: Giorgio di Sant'Angelo,
Shredded gown, ca. 1969

Pages 116–17: Giorgio di Sant'Angelo,
Shredded gown (detail), ca. 1969

Page 118: Christian Francis Roth,
American hobo suit,
fall/winter 1991–92

GLOSSARY

Banyan: man's loose coat, falling to the knee, worn informally in the seventeenth and eighteenth centuries.

Busk: in the traditional corset, a spine slotted in the front that holds the torso erect; generally of whalebone, horn, ivory, or even steel.

Camisole: in the nineteenth century, a bed jacket or loose corset; by the end of that century, the camisole had become an unstructured underbodice.

Chemise: the sleeveless knee-length garment worn as underclothing in the eighteenth century; later, a description of the same silhouette, especially in the 1920s.

Chemisette: in the nineteenth century, the pared-down underbodice or fill-in that often shows at a low-cut neckline.

Chemise à la reine: the chemise as worn externally first by Marie Antoinette in the 1780s and prevailing as a style into the Empire. It was also fostered by children's dress: the girl could wear the chemise into adolescence; the child of nature could wear it forever.

Combing jacket: woman's loose jacket (late nineteenth and into the twentieth century) as derived from dressing gowns, but generally only waist-length, worn in the bedroom when brushing the hair or applying makeup.

Corset: a stiff shaping garment of the torso, tending to pronounced diminution of the waist and raising of the bust. A variant was used by men as well.

Crinoline: a cage-like structure of hoops giving wide circumference to the skirt. The diameter of the hoops increases from top to bottom, creating a cone-like shape. The word derives from *crin* (horsehair) and *lin* (petticoat linen).

Girdle: by the 1920s, a rubberized and elasticized variation on the corset, covering the upper thigh as well.

Hoop: understructure to carry petticoats and clothing in wide circumference around the body, generally from waist to feet in graduated enlargement.

Lingerie: originally, the French for linen products, but more broadly taken to mean luxury undergarments and sleepwear in the nineteenth century. A generic term, it served to legitimize "unmentionables," undergarments that propriety was too modest to describe, though its connotation is specifically of better-quality intimate apparel.

Merry Widow: a 1951 corset manufactured by Warner's and named after the operetta by Franz Lehár. A pronounced hourglass shape, it corresponded to the New Look shaping, restraining the waist and lifting the bust.

Morning dress: modified, yet informal, dressing for women in the home in the nineteenth century, taking its name from the time of day prior to social visiting and formal ceremonies.

Negligee: literally neglected, the attire of privacy and informality.

Petticoat: in the Renaissance, the petticoat was an external garment; in the nineteenth century, perhaps in Renaissance revival, the term was reused to describe underskirts, often worn layered.

Robe de chambre: initially, men's deshabille attire in the eighteenth century; later, women's informal dress, including morning gowns and wrappers.

Robe volante: an eighteenth-century gown with loosely fitted bodice and box pleats at the back.

Sack (Sacque): a capacious gown like a belled tent with pleats at neckband, worn as an open robe both for dress and undress after 1750.

Slip: a light undergarment suspended from the shoulders and extending to the hem of the skirt. (In the twentieth century, a half slip describes a garment hanging from the waist.) Often an interface between an inner layer of undergarment and external clothing, the slip is an intermediary: it occasionally appears through to the outer layer and, with the twentieth-century slip dress, it becomes the outer layer of clothing.

Tea gown: an uncorseted gown of informality; by the 1920s, a semi-formal attire of the same type suitable for garden parties and afternoon tea.

Underskirt: a layered garment. In the Renaissance, an underskirt could be of the same fabrics as external dress and sometimes shows through, as in the blue underskirt worn in Jan van Eyck's *The Marriage of Giovanni and Jeanne Arnolfini* (1434); in modern use, it is a petticoat or similar undergarment.

Wrapper: an informal wraparound robe with easy tying worn at home. Twentieth-century derivations from the wrapper for women include the housedress and housecoat.

SELECTED BIBLIOGRAPHY

Carter, Alison. *Underwear: The Fashion History,* New York, 1992.

Cunningham, Patricia A. "Eighteenth Century Nightgowns: The Gentleman's Robe in Art and Fashion," *Dress,* X, 1984, pp. 2–11.

Cunnington, C. W. and Phillis. *The History of Underclothes,* Rev. ed., Boston, 1981.

Ewing, Elizabeth. *Dress and Undress: A History of Women's Underwear,* New York, 1978.

Hollander, Anne. *Seeing Through Clothes,* New York, 1978.

Fashion Institute of Technology and Kyoto Costume Institute. *The Undercover Story,* New York, 1982.

Kunzle, David. *Fashion and Fetishism: A Social History of the Corset, Tight-Lacing and Other Forms of Body-Sculpture in the West,* Totowa, New Jersey, 1982.

Libron, Fernand and Clouzot, Henri. *Le Corset dans l'Art et les Moeurs du XIIIe au XXe Siecle,* Paris, 1933.

Perrot, Philippe. *Les Dessus et Les Dessous de la Bourgeoisie: Une Histoire du Vetement au XIXe Siecle,* Paris, 1981.

Probert, Christina. *Lingerie in Vogue since 1910,* New York, 1981.

Ribeiro, Aileen. *Dress and Morality,* London, 1986.

Rudofsky, Bernard. *The Unfashionable Human Body,* New York, 1971.

Saint Laurent, Cecil. *A History of Women's Underwear,* London, 1986.

Waugh, Norah. *Corsets and Crinolines,* London, 1954.

LIST OF ILLUSTRATIONS

All costume photographs are by Neil Selkirk, unless otherwise indicated.

Cover: Fendi, *Corset bathing suit,* spring/summer 1991, white nylon Spandex. Courtesy Anna Fendi

Incongruous and anachronistic, the Fendi bathing suit is a tour de force of historical acuity and irony. If the corset once oppressed women and suppressed movement, a contemporary swimsuit can only serve as an unconditional sign of motion and physical liberation.

Frontispiece: French, *Robe volante,* ca. 1735–40, brown silk damask. The Metropolitan Museum of Art. Gift of Mary Tavener Holmes, 1983 (1983.399.1)

The informal *robe volante* became an important option to the formal dress of the eighteenth century as its structure cleaved to a tailor's standard.

Page 5: Gabrielle Chanel, *Evening ensemble,* 1939, black and white silk net, white cotton eyelet, and multicolored, striped silk taffeta sash. The Metropolitan Museum of Art, Gift of Mrs. John Chambers Hughes, 1958 (CI 58.34.18)

Evidence of lingerie's abiding allure to clothing, the Chanel evening ensemble represents a repertoire of lingerie techniques and surprising reversals and revelations; a crinoline as overskirt and an underslip revealed. Chanel's ironies are highly informed; her reinterpretations of lingerie are purposely unseemly and richly elegant.

Page 6: Josie Natori, left: *Slip dress,* fall/winter 1990–91, black re-embroidered and beaded lace with nude underdress. Courtesy Josie Natori; right: *Baby doll dress,* spring/summer 1990, black silk chiffon with black re-embroidered stretch lace underdress. Courtesy Josie Natori

Known as a designer of intimate apparel, Josie Natori was encouraged in the 1980s by Lynn Manulis of Martha to bring her sensibility and technical prowess to daywear and evening wear inspired by lingerie.

Page 9: Jean Paul Gaultier, *"Express Yourself"* ensemble, 1990, black chalk striped wool suit with pink satin and elastic corset. Courtesy Madonna

Page 12: Attributed to Élisabeth Vigée-Lebrun, *Marie Antoinette,* ca. 1783, oil on canvas. National Gallery of Art, Washington, D.C., Timken Collection (1960.6.41)

The startling innocence of Marie Antoinette's decision to wear and to be depicted in the chemise was a revolutionary gesture, a clothing transformation notably in advance of the Revolution, but an ominous precursor of the chemise worn on last rides on the tumbrel. Was there not an anticipation of democratic reform in shedding the silk shell of Court dress?

Page 15: Follower of Jacques-Louis David, *Portrait of a Young Woman in White,* ca. 1800, oil on canvas. National Gallery of Art, Washington, D.C., Chester Dale Collection (1963.10.118)

The American Rosalie Stier Calvert reports in her letters in 1802 of a Betsy Cooke of whom "it is believed that she will die from a cold she caught at a ball where she wore a Greek dress," the peril of the new style. Further, Calvert reports in the same year, "Papa recently came back [from the city] and couldn't stop talking about two ladies who he said reminded him of eels stripped of their skin—without skirt, sleeves, or anything to furnish them some grace," her father apparently finding scant grace in the new neoclassicism.

Page 16: American, *Dress,* 1799–1800, white linen with foliate embroidery. The Metropolitan Museum of Art, Purchase, Irene Lewisohn and Alice L. Crowley Bequests, 1988 (1988.242.4)

The Empire Style gave solemnity and classical reason to the simple linen dress that had been only an undergarment a generation before. Already, though, decoration is beginning in foliate embroidery, betokening a first stage in the nineteenth-century *horror vacui* vis-a-vis clothing embellishment.

Page 21: Alfred Stieglitz, *Mrs. Selma Schubart* (Stieglitz's sister Selma), 1907, lumiere autochrome. The Metropolitan Museum of Art, Gift of Georgia O'Keeffe, 1955 (55.635.14)

Still private, even as a family photograph, Stieglitz's image of his sister wearing a Fortuny gown implies both artistic progressivism and naturalism in a garden setting.

Pages 22–23: Mariano Fortuny, *Delphos dresses,* silk. The Metropolitan Museum of Art. Top left and clockwise: ca. 1920. Purchase, Isabel Shults Fund, 1984 (1984.609a); first half of the twentieth century. Gift of Claudia Lyon, 1974 (1974.339a); ca. 1930. Gift of the Estate of Agnes Miles Carpenter, 1958 (CI 58.61.4); ca. 1920–30. Gift of Gloria Braggiotti, 1980 (1980.170); first third of the twentieth century. Gift of Irene Lewisohn and Alice Lewisohn Crowley, 1946 (CI 46.9.82); ca. 1950. Gift of the Duchess Pini di San Miniato, 1980 (1980.186a); 1939. Gift of the Family of Mrs. M. Lincoln Schuster, 1977 (1977.363.14); 1936. Gift of Dorothy M. Fordyce, 1983 (1983.477a); early twentieth century. Gift of Mrs. Francis Coleman and Mrs. Charles H. Erhart, Jr., 1975 (1975.383.4)

Intended as apparel with one circumscribed, though important, use as a tea gown, the Fortuny Delphos came to be used as a distinctive style in evening wear. Marcel Proust wrote, "Of all the indoor and outdoor gowns that Mme de Guermantes wore, those which seemed most to respond to a definite intention, to be endowed with a special significance, were the garments made by Fortuny from old Venetian models."

Page 25: Cristobal Balenciaga, *Baby doll dress,* 1957, black silk lace. The Metropolitan Museum of Art, Gift of Mrs. T. Reed Vreeland, 1973 (1973.20)

The baby doll dress is a feat of legerdemain, wrapping the body in a comfortable form, but allowing the lace cage to swing free. While other couture designers copied the baby doll dress, its perfect form was found in Balenciaga, whose life-long interest in the contrast of embrace and loose swing was distilled in this form.

Page 26: Geoffrey Beene, *Spiral slip dress,* 1991, black wool jersey, point d'esprit, and marquisette rosettes. Courtesy Jonee Sopher

Beene's couture-standard perfectionism is manifest in the exacting fit and sheer audacity of the slip dress. A tour de force of dressmaking technique accompanied by consummate lingerie skills, the Beene slip dress is commensurate with the couture of Vionnet.

Page 27: Claire McCardell, *Evening gown,* 1950, umber satin-striped nylon. Courtesy Fashion Institute of Technology, Gift of Mrs. Adrian McCardell

The humble (and in 1950, quite new) material of nylon is raised by McCardell to evening-wear stature in a neoclassical, very modern, gown. McCardell had also used cotton piqué and other unexpected materials for evening wear, granting a kind of natural democracy to fabrics.

Page 29: Pablo Picasso, *Girl in a Chemise,* 1905. Tate Gallery, London/Art Resource, New York © ARS, New York/SPADEM, Paris

For Picasso, the chemise suggests a number of interpretations: simplicity and even poverty; a *regressus ad originem* of the chemise as a kind of primal shift; a basic attire of daywear and nightwear.

Page 31: Jacques-Louis David, *Antoine Laurent Lavoisier and His Wife,* 1788, oil on canvas. The Metropolitan Museum of Art, Purchase, Mr. and Mrs. Charles Wrightsman Gift, in honor of Everett Fahy, 1977 (1977.10)

Almost immediately in the 1780s, the underwear that was coming to the surface was supported by the volume-bearing understructure that had characterized eighteenth-century dress. Mme Lavoisier's dress is thus transitional: it exposes the devices of underwear but maintains a traditional structure.

Page 32: J.-F. de Troy, *The Declaration of Love,* 1724. Private collection, New York

In an intimate setting, a relative state of déshabille signals the presence of love. The *robe volante*'s undress origins are even more explicit in the circumstance of unloosed stays.

Page 34: John Singleton Copley, *Joseph Sherburne,* ca. 1767–70, oil on canvas. The Metropolitan Museum of Art, Amelia B. Lazarus Fund, 1923 (23.143)

The custom of showing the eighteenth-century gentleman in the relaxed style of the banyan gives narrative and character to the sitter, suggesting a kind of humanism and an approachable, friendly style.

Page 35: European, *Man's banyan*, ca. 1780, blue, ivory, rust, and yellow striped silk satin. The Metropolitan Museum of Art, Purchase, Irene Lewisohn Bequest, 1956 (CI 56.5.1)

The sign of an eighteenth-century man at ease, the banyan was a comfortable and frequently colorful style for men of the Court and of affairs. Collegians in the eighteenth century adopted the same style for public places in the spirit of adolescent informality and rebellion, and they were denounced for appearing in their nightgowns.

Page 37: Raimundo de Madrazo y Garreta, *Girls at a Window*, n.d., oil on canvas. The Metropolitan Museum of Art, Catharine Lorillard Wolfe Collection, Bequest of Catharine Lorillard Wolfe, 1887 (87.15.131)

In twentieth-century art, the window is metaphor and frame to the real world. In the nineteenth century, figures appear in windows as they would have in the new urbanism of such sites as Haussmann's Paris, but with the interaction between the private interior and the public boulevard and spectatorship. Such figures are at the uncertain threshold between two modes.

Page 39: Édouard Manet, *Woman with a Parrot* (detail), n.d., oil on canvas. The Metropolitan Museum of Art, Gift of Erwin Davis, 1889 (89.21.3)

Manet depicted every stage of dress and undress, often in juxtaposition with another person or persons at a different stage. While he is indubitably the shrewd observer of dress as a process, Manet also measures decency, dress, undress, the dressing gown, and shock through the graduated presences he gives to clothing.

Page 41: Yves Saint Laurent for Christian Dior, *Evening dress*, spring/summer 1960, pale green silk shantung. The Metropolitan Museum of Art, Gift of Baron Philippe de Rothschild, 1983 (1983.619.8)

What had been a dressing gown for Manet's *Woman with a Parrot* is appropriated by Saint Laurent for Christian Dior as an evening dress. Saint Laurent's allusions to art are frequent, including the *Mondrian dress* (1965), Matisse collection (fall/winter 1981–82), and Van Gogh and Cubist derivations (the late 1980s). Most significant, though, in conjunction with this Manet-inspired dress are the Goya-inspired dresses Saint Laurent created for Dior during the following season, fall/winter 1960–61.

Page 42: Karl Lagerfeld for Chanel, *Evening ensemble*, 1992, white ribbed cotton tank top, black silk tulle skirt, and metal and faux tortoise link belt. Courtesy Chanel

Lagerfeld has perpetuated and extended Chanel's knack for editorial judgment from the street and vernacular clothing. In this instance, Lagerfeld creates the high form of clothing that began as underwear, sought fashion associations through designer labels, and is finally fulfilled in its ambition as it is dismayingly expropriated by the designer's passion for contradiction.

Page 43: *Marky Mark [Mark Wahlberg]*, 1993. Photograph by Herb Ritts for Calvin Klein, photograph courtesy Calvin Klein

In the 1990s, an urban street style of loose jeans worn low on the hips exposed the waistbands of briefs, themselves vested in the 1980s and 1990s with designer identities. Singer Marky Mark, known first for dropping his trousers in concerts, became a very familiar body in Calvin Klein advertising.

Page 45: Édouard Manet, *Nana*, 1877. Kunsthalle, Hamburg

By the 1860s, silk-surfaced corsets were developed. By the 1870s, embroidered satin corsets introduced elements of luxury and secret indulgence. *Nana* is preparing for her tournure or bustle, decorative overpetticoat, and dress: we see an early stage in the dressing process.

Page 46: Georges Seurat, *Jeune fille se poudrant*, 1888–90, oil on canvas. Courtauld Institute Galleries, London (Courtauld gift)

Minimalizing the waist causes secondary displacements of flesh made evident by Seurat: a pronounced bust line, an erect posture with a plumbline effect of the corset on the spine, and exaggerated hip line. Seurat's sense of the verticality and volumes of the human figure is evident throughout his painting: in seeing the figure in a corset, we see that Seurat's axiality of pose is founded in the corset.

Page 49: Henri de Toulouse-Lautrec, *Femme à sa toilette*, 1896. Musée des Augustins, Toulouse

An artist of the modern sites and conditions of spectatorship, Toulouse-Lautrec provides the bifocal witness of the art's spectator and the male viewer within the scene. The male viewer's gaze insinuates its proximate voyeurism into the spectator's point of view, making palpable the watchful fetishism of regarding the dressing process and observing the lacing of the corset.

Page 51: *Madonna*, 1990, wearing Jean Paul Gaultier, *"Like a Virgin" corset*, 1990, gold-sprayed lamé. Courtesy Madonna. Photograph by Jean Baptiste Mondino, photograph courtesy Jean Baptiste Mondino and *Harper's Bazaar*

Madonna has been a critical figure in the contemporary phenomenon of *Infra-Apparel,* choosing costume that is historically reactionary while at the same time aggressively vanguard. Madonna has worn underwear as performance clothing since the early 1980s.

Page 52: Gianni Versace, *Corset gown,* fall/winter 1991–92, white silk crepe and white silk ottoman. Courtesy Gianni Versace

A designer of encyclopedic referencing and intense popular-culture energy, Versace creates a gown from the traditional paradigm of the corset.

Page 53: Gianni Versace, left: *Slip dress,* fall/winter 1991–92, powder blue silk crepe, chiffon, and lace. Courtesy Gianni Versace; right: *Baby doll dress,* fall/winter 1991–92, pink silk crepe, faille, chiffon, and lace. Courtesy Gianni Versace

Re-creating historical types, Versace imbues each with a contemporary fervor akin to Pop Art hyperbole. Versace makes us aware of the exemplar through an exaggerated version, verging on the caricature. Thus, an almost scholastic taxonomy of clothing types becomes for Versace an audacious suite of slightly spoofy, highly original variations.

Page 55: Yves Saint Laurent, left: *Corset dress,* fall/winter 1991–92, black lace over nude silk chiffon, black silk georgette and lace skirt, with black tulle and velvet trim. Courtesy Yves Saint Laurent; right: *Corset dress,* fall/winter 1991–92, black silk velvet and lace with satin ribbon embroidered lace trim. Courtesy Yves Saint Laurent

The corsetry revived by Saint Laurent in the 1990s recalls the Belle Epoque in a gesture of the designer's characteristically post-modern historicism. One fin de siècle recalls another.

Page 56: Thierry Mugler, *Corset suit,* fall/winter 1992–93, red wool crepe jacket with black cotton velvet skirt. Courtesy Thierry Mugler

The *tailleur* of a Mugler corset suit consolidates innerwear and external clothing indissolubly.

Page 57: Belville Sassoon, *Evening bodice,* ca. 1985, shown with Perry Ellis skirt in leopard patterned taffeta. Courtesy Mrs. Robert S. Trump

The lacing of the bodice is unusual in exposing the torso. While the shape seems very restraining in the corset tradition, the suppleness of the velvet transforms the traditional form into a softer modern attire.

Page 58: Jacques Fath, *Evening gown,* 1947, pink silk satin. Courtesy Richard Martin

Pink, a color of twentieth-century lingerie, is combined by Fath with traditional lacing in an evening gown of tight-laced eroticism. Its structure is a literal equivalent of the hourglass silhouette of the post-World War II years, here given deeper historical resonance. In 1954, just before his death, Fath returned to the representation of the corset as a means of rationalizing the wasp waist he preferred.

Page 59: Jacques Fath, *Evening gown* (detail), 1947

Page 60: Valentino [Garavani], *Evening gown,* fall/winter 1992–93, red silk crepe and quilted silk satin. Courtesy Valentino

Valentino knowingly re-creates the quilting of 1820s and 1830s corsets that extend to the hip, playing upon that historical style as a cuirass on an evening gown. Quilting and decorative pattern give the corset element its intercessory role between evening gown and carapace. Further, he emphasizes the graceful symmetry of the body with ties at center front.

Page 61: Jean Paul Gaultier, *Evening dress,* 1992, black rayon satin and Lycra. Courtesy Richard Martin.

Inspired by the 1950s Merry Widow, the Gaultier evening dress is one of numerous instances of the designer's love of brazen exposure. His metal corset, burlesque conical bras, and suite of historicizing corsets represent one aspect of Gaultier's deft and often droll displacements of clothing templates.

Page 63: F. X. Winterhalter, *Mme Rimsky-Korsakov,* 1864. Musée d'Orsay, Paris. © Photo R.M.N.

The body-conscious, self-aware Mme Rimsky-Korsakov may make a deliberate choice to be represented in deshabille, but her attire is very similar to that of other Second Empire portraits of women fully dressed. Shared elements include: taffeta ribbons channeled through gathered white organza, lace, and shirred white fabric.

Page 67: F. X. Winterhalter, *Elizabeth, Empress of Austria,* 1864. Location unknown. Photograph National Portrait Gallery, London

In a sense, Elizabeth of Austria anticipated the modern interest in dieting, exercise, and the mystique of health. Her portrait in undress is an essay in rationality and physical continence. She is not the *coquette,* but a modern Diana of the healthy, chaste, and functional in underwear. The public expectation for such a portrait would have been formality; it scandalized not only because of its intimacy, but also because of its austerity.

Pages 68–69: F. X. Winterhalter, *Empress Eugénie and Her Ladies of Honor,* 1855, oil on canvas. Musée National du Château, Compiègne. Giraudon/Art Resource, New York

The lavish dress of the period was a finery for the court, though some critics and cynics noted the similarity to the florid dress of courtesans, as earlier had been charged in the exposure of lingerie motives.

Page 70: French, *Wedding dress,* 1864, white cotton organdy with whitework embroidery. The Metropolitan Museum of Art, Gift of Mrs. James Sullivan, 1926 (26.250.2)

The bride's gown and trousseau were imbued with virginal values and the delight of lingerie forms peeking through in public. The mid-nineteenth-century wedding dress was both raw and cooked: it carried the solemnity of a rite of passage, but with the exuberance and extravagance of ancient and feral forms.

Page 71: American, *Corset covers and combing jackets,* late nineteenth century, white linen, cotton Valenciennes lace, and whitework embroidered muslin. The Metropolitan Museum of Art, Gift of Mrs. V. P. Delgado-Orth and Mrs. V. J. Hill, 1946 (46.91.4); Gift of Mrs. William Rosenfeld, 1943 (43.113.13); Gift of Mrs. Harry Allan Jacobs, 1938 (CI 38.50.1)

Whitework techniques were among the most elaborate style grammars of the nineteenth century, suggesting eclectic sources, aesthetic diversity in a sumptuous form, and the precious survival of ancient techniques. Pictured in this way, these items of intimate clothing are the textile twin to Owen Jones's *Grammar of Ornament* or other stylebooks and patternbooks.

Page 72: American, *Petticoats,* 1880–1907, white organdy, whitework embroidered muslin, silk taffeta, cotton Valenciennes lace, and corded net. The Metropolitan Museum of Art, Gift of Mrs. Arthur Bloch, 1940 (40.149). Gift of Mrs. Edwin J. Gutman, 1944 (44.93.11). Gift of Mrs. Edgar L. Rossin, 1953 (CI 53.12)

With the invention of the bobbinet machine by John Heathcoat, the labor-intensive handmaking of lace was superfluous. Ironically, handmade lace proliferated after the availability of machine-made lace as a willful act of sabotage and social atavism. Perhaps the indulgence in the technique (and manual virtuosity) could be enjoyed more as soon as the Industrial Revolution provided a machine alternative.

Page 73: American, *Reception dress,* late 1870s, ivory silk organza and lace with silk satin ribbon trim. Courtesy Richard Martin

A plethora of opulent techniques attached themselves to the white dresses of the second half of the nineteenth century. Cascades of drapery were integrated into the body of the dress to freeze the tumbling away of cloth implied by deshabille.

Page 75: American, *Lingerie dress,* ca. 1877, white cotton batiste. The Metropolitan Museum of Art, The Jacqueline Loewe Fowler Costume Collection, Gift of Jacqueline Loewe Fowler, 1981 (1981.380.1)

An American lingerie dress with train exhibits the tour de force of technical capabilities that were on display as lingerie and exterior dress exchanged roles and mastery in the last quarter of the nineteenth century.

Page 76: European, *Dress* (detail), ca. 1818, white cotton with white lace and white mull trim. The Metropolitan Museum of Art, Purchase, Marcia Sand Bequest in memory of her daughter Tiger (Joan) Morse, 1981 (1981.13.3)

The first justification of the chemise was a neoclassicism, but its perpetuation depended upon the adaptability of such white dresses to be a tabula rasa to historical styles, taking on the attributes of the waves of historicism that washed over the decades of the nineteenth century.

Page 77: American, *Dress,* early 1840s, white cotton organdy. The Metropolitan Museum of Art, Gift of the Art Workers' Club, 1945 (CI 45.68.28)

Lace insets, whitework embroidery, and shirred banding became a trinity of nineteenth-century ornament quoted by lingerie. The dress-underwear exchange of motives in the nineteenth century is in some ways similar to the visual exchange between printmaking and painting in the same period.

Page 79: left: English, *Day dress,* ca. 1833–34, white cotton embroidered with lily-of-the-valley motif. The Metropolitan Museum of Art, Purchase, Irene Lewisohn Trust Fund, 1981 (1981.118.3); right: American, *Day dress,* ca. 1842, white lawn embroidered with foliate pattern. The Metropolitan Museum of Art, Gift of The New-York Historical Society, 1979 (1979.346.41)

As in these dresses, decoration on lingerie of the first half of the nineteenth century was largely restricted to whitework embroidery at the neckline, sleeves, and hem.

Pages 80–81: American, *Dress* (detail), 1840s, white cotton with articulated boned bodice. The Metropolitan Museum of Art, Promised gift of Richard Martin and Harold Koda in honor of Cora Ginsburg

In this dress, modernism speaks in advance of its time. The decoration emulates structure, the pattern of the bodice resembling the corset. The anonymous American *Dress* anticipates the cool reason and analytical historicism of such twentieth-century work as Bill Blass's *Evening dress* (see p. 92).

Page 83: French, *Wedding dress* (detail), ca. 1837, white India muslin with embroidered floral motif. The Metropolitan Museum of Art, Gift of Mrs. R. T. Auchmuty, 1915 (15.149.1)

Detachable sheer sleeves cage the interior sleeve and provide an outer layer of ornament and form for the structure beneath, a Crystal Palace in muslin.

Page 84: left: American, *Semi-evening dress,* ca. 1903–4, off-white silk mull with cotton Valenciennes lace. The Metropolitan Museum of Art, Gift of Miss Finn, 1946 (46.10.7); right: American, *Afternoon dress,* ca. 1908, cream silk with cotton lace and cotton point d'esprit. The Metropolitan Museum of Art, Gift of Estate of Helen F. Swan, 1975 (1975.55)

Early twentieth-century dress liberally quoted silk lingerie of the 1880s and 1890s.

Page 85: American, *Semi-evening dress* (detail), ca. 1903–4

Page 86: Boué Soeurs, *Robe de style,* ca. 1920, white embroidered lawn, filet lace, cotton net, and silk ribbon rosettes. Courtesy Mark Walsh

Notable as creators of lingerie, as Callot Soeurs had been as a lace establishment, Boué Soeurs carried the materials and ornament of lingerie to dressmaking.

Page 87: Boué Soeurs, *Robe de style* (detail), ca. 1920

Page 89: left: Lucile, *Dress,* ca. 1912, cream silk chiffon with cotton lace and corded net. The Metropolitan Museum of Art, Gift of Mrs. Morton E. Snellenburg, 1946 (46.46.6); right: Lucile, *Tea dance dress,* ca. 1916–17, white marquisette with lace and ribbon trim. The Metropolitan Museum of Art, Gift of Julia B. Henry, 1978 (1978.288.1)

Lingerie-like materials and the garment's transparency afford the same effect in dress as in lingerie, fostering an ambiguity of layers seductive in both.

Pages 90–91: Lucile, *Tea dance dress* (detail), ca. 1916–17

Page 92: Bill Blass, *Evening dress,* ca. 1987, pink pintucked silk. Courtesy Mary Tavener Holmes Berry

Pintucking is a technical device for fit. The Blass dress uses pintucking less structurally than decoratively, evoking the sleek bias of dressing gowns of the 1930s.

Page 93: Bergdorf Goodman, *Evening dress and jacket,* 1938, beige silk marquisette and cotton lace. The Metropolitan Museum of Art, Gift of Mrs. Alan L. Corey, Jr., Mrs. William T. Newbold, and Mrs. A. G. Paine II, 1980 (1980.126.7)

The cosmetic colors of intimate apparel transferred in many instances to evening wear.

Page 95: Comme des Garçons, *Day ensembles,* 1981, left: white cotton jersey T-shirt with taping appliqués over a cotton jersey and cloth patchwork skirt; right: white cotton jersey and cloth T-shirt over a cotton jersey and cloth skirt with taping appliqués. Photograph by Peter Lindbergh for Comme des Garçons, 1983. Courtesy Comme des Garçons

Rei Kawakubo's design for Comme des Garçons in the early 1980s was as picturesque as London Punk, but more structurally aware.

Page 99: Comme des Garçons, *Lace sweater,* fall/winter 1982–83, black wool, coordinated with a black cotton jersey padded skirt. Photograph by Peter Lindbergh for Comme des Garçons, 1982. Courtesy Comme des Garçons

Rei Kawakubo's design of the lace sweater occasioned a fashion of privilege, immediately separating a responsive audience of approval and outcry against the work. A happy few acknowledged the work, understanding that its principle was not destruction but affirmation. To many others in the early 1980s, of course, the Comme des Garçons work seemed cryptic, apocalyptic, or sociopathological.

Page 103: Martin Margiela, *"Lining" dress,* 1991, white viscose. *Shoulder structure,* spring/summer, 1991, washed cotton. *Jabot,* spring/summer, 1989, washed cotton. *"Japanese Workman" shoes,* spring/summer, 1989. Photograph by Martin Margiela. Courtesy Martin Margiela

Calling him "the pioneer whose time has come" (*New York Times,* March 16, 1991), Bernadine Morris noted Margiela's deconstructivist clothing and sensibility. While wholly finished, Margiela's works suggest process and a systematic, somewhat radical, reconsideration of all the tenets of apparel.

Page 107: Madeleine Vionnet, *Honeycomb dress,* 1936, black silk organza with pintucking. The Metropolitan Museum of Art, Gift of Mrs. John Chambers Hughes, 1958 (CI 58.34.15)

What *Mont Saint Victoire* was to Cézanne, the dress is to Vionnet, a designer of infinitely analytical patience and introspection. Borrowing broadly from the techniques of innerwear, Vionnet created analytical structures hidden beneath webs, dexterous excisions and modifications, and, in this case, a honeycomb on a dress. The result is a dress that is sensitively elegant and as ontological as a garment can be, its visual refinement emanating from its problem-solving reason.

Page 108: Jeanne Lanvin, *Evening gown* (detail), 1937–39

Page 109: Jeanne Lanvin, *Evening gown,* 1937–39, black silk satin and net with hoop panniers. The Metropolitan Museum of Art, Gift of Mrs. Stephen M. Kellen, 1978 (1978.165.19)

Once known chiefly for a ladylike sensibility, Lanvin is increasingly revealed as a designer of discriminating interest in structure and of keen historical awareness. The hoops of this dress return to the eighteenth century.

Page 110: Marc Jacobs for Perry Ellis, *Tear gown,* 1993, black rayon Lycra jersey with reversed seams. Courtesy Perry Ellis

Jacobs is an unabashed fan of Elsa Schiaparelli. His *Tear gown* recalls Schiaparelli's *"Tear"* gown (1938), but offers a third possibility (to Schiaparelli's dress and veil techniques) of actual tears in the garment. Jacobs's smart knowledge of design history, quick and instinctive referencing of cultural issues, and propensity to the literary and intellectual dimension of fashion mark work that includes picnic-table etiquettes, a Freudian slip, subtle homage to Perry Ellis, and a *Hugs dress* (1986), also a tribute to Schiaparelli of the 1930s.

Page 111: Issey Miyake, *Print and cut jacket,* fall/winter 1992–93, ivory alpaca and mohair felt with black pigment-printed pattern line. Courtesy Jun Kanai

Caroline Rennolds Milbank claims in *Couture,* "with Miyake we have come back to the time when the couturier/designer provides the client with cloth to be used in any way the client sees fit," thus recognizing Miyake's respect for the integrity of textiles and the possibility of basic clothing shapes. Always the geometer, Miyake is as sensitive to deconstruction as he is to the forms of textiles.

Pages 112–13: Karl Lagerfeld for Fendi, *Deconstructed fur coat* (detail), fall/winter 1992–93, green sheared muskrat with perforated green micro-fiber shell. Courtesy Fendi

A reversed and rent fur coat revokes all the superficial associations with the form. Lagerfeld dramatically annuls all that is expected of the fur coat when its structure is exposed and faces transposed. Of course, the structure bespeaks a new, unexpected beauty perhaps even greater than the conventional and age-old resplendence of fur.

Page 115: Giorgio di Sant'Angelo, *Shredded gown,* ca. 1969, suede with multicolored silk chiffon. Courtesy Martin Price

Sant'Angelo's reference to Native Americans may justify in part his defiant break with the modern idea of the integrity of the garment, but it in no way mitigates the surprise of the modern spectator on seeing a garment so much like the scraps and tatters that are conventionally seen as clothing's detritus, not its condition of beauty.

Pages 116–17: Giorgio di Sant'Angelo, *Shredded gown* (detail), ca. 1969

Page 118: Christian Francis Roth, *American hobo suit,* fall/winter 1991–92, red wool with multicolored wool insets. Courtesy Lynn Manulis

Roth is a fashion dreamer, adroitly placing his work in a picturesque style. Thematic, highly cohesive collections by Roth are as much a semi-annual credo as they are a suite of paintings—or, in this instance, their fashion counterpart—that suggest an evocative theme, such as American innocence, a grunge pastoral, the romance of France, or Surrealist recollection.

Page 129: left: Callot Soeurs, *Underslip,* ca. 1927, apricot silk chiffon and ecru Valenciennes lace; center: Callot Soeurs, *Evening dress,* ca. 1927, peach silk, point d'esprit, gilt corded lace, and satin ribbon rosettes; right: Callot Soeurs, *Underslip,* ca. 1927, pale orange silk, marquisette, and gilt blond lace. Courtesy Martin Kamer

The underslips of Callot Soeurs have all the construction and components of the dress with the exception of the modesty of a liner. The dress has all the techniques and embellishments of peignoirs, nightgowns, and underslips.

Page 129: Callot Soeurs, left: *Underslip,* ca. 1927; center: *Evening dress,* ca. 1927; right: *Underslip,* ca. 1927

ACKNOWLEDGMENTS

These recognitions are inevitably too modest in scale for the individuals and institutions contributing in many and invaluable ways to *Infra-Apparel*. While the core of the exhibition comes from The Costume Institute, loans have made possible the full survey of historical and contemporary materials. We are grateful to generous designers: Geoffrey Beene and Richard Lambertson, Geoffrey Beene; Anne Fahey and Arlette Thébault, Chanel; Marion Greenberg and Jody Quon, Comme des Garçons; Laura Danford, Perry Ellis; Anna Fendi, Anna Mariani, and Albert Morris, Fendi; Kelly Klein and Michelle Kessler, Calvin Klein; Else Skalvoll, Martin Margiela; Anna Cosentino, Thierry Mugler; Josie and Ken Natori and Jeanette Chai Cantone, Natori; Christian Francis Roth; Martin Price, Giorgio di Sant'Angelo; Joy Hendricks and Christophe Gérard, Yves Saint Laurent; Bruce Hoeksema, Robin Nord, Georgelina Stanicich and Judy Lance, Valentino. Private lenders have helped us immensely: Tav Holmes Berry, Martin Kamer, Jun Kanai, Lynn Manulis, Jonee Sopher, Mrs. Robert S. Trump, and Mark Walsh. We are grateful for the special cooperation of Madonna, Darlene K. Lutz, Liz Rosenberg, and Christine Wolff. Our former colleague and longtime friend Ellen Shanley assisted us at the Fashion Institute of Technology.

We gladly acknowledge friends who gave generously and personally in inimitable ways to *Infra-Apparel*: Cora Ginsburg, Titi Halle, and Donna Ghelerter of Cora Ginsburg were faithful counsel and incomparable resources; Harriet Weintraub has been our friend and wonderful partisan; Gianni Versace was characteristically obliging and enterprising; Rose Simon gave, as always, with infectious enthusiasm and knowledgeable interest; Josie and Ken Natori have provided sponsorship for the *Infra-Apparel* exhibition in objectivity, but also in a shared belief in the idea that clothing can effectively, even beautifully, mediate privacy and public demeanor.

Colleagues in The Costume Institute of The Metropolitan Museum of Art made worthy contributions to *Infra-Apparel*. Chris Paulocik, assisted by Rita Kauneckas, brought refreshing vitality to all the garments photographed and in the exhibition; Beth Alberty, Lillian Dickler, Deirdre Donahue, Kimberly S. Fink, Joell Kunath, Jennifer Loveman, Michele Majer, Dennita Sewell, and Jason Weller have helped give the exhibition physical and intellectual form. Katell le Bourhis continues to sustain us, even from far away, as our friend and paragon.

This book was created with the extraordinary vision of Neil Selkirk and Yolanda Cuomo. The sensitivity of their photography and art direction gives the book its allure and discriminating vision. It has been a special privilege to work with two such creative talents. Our editorial team of John P. O'Neill, Barbara Burn, Barbara Cavaliere, and Peter Antony perforce became better friends than one could imagine in the space of two months. It is a friendship we will always value and strive to merit. In fact, we two tenderfeet have depended upon the experts at The Metropolitan Museum of Art. What we have, in fact, depended upon is more than mere proficiency; we have enjoyed a liberal and affirming generosity of spirit from Philippe de Montebello, Bill Luers, Penny Bardel, Ashton Hawkins, Emily Rafferty, Harold Holzer, Dick Morsches, Jeff Daley, Linda Sylling, and Phylis Fogelson. They have been more than overseers and colleagues: they have been gentle companions and new fast friends, even to the freshest, most accident-prone curators.

One joy in coming to the Metropolitan is the cooperation we enjoy with the Museum's estimable circle of supporters; Mrs. William F. Buckley, Jr. and the Visiting Committee of The Costume Institute have been consummate friends and a wonderful support; Eleanor Lambert, so instrumental in our coming to the Museum, has been our continuing friend and mentor.

Infra-Apparel is, admittedly, a proposition. We have purposefully chosen to begin a campaign of exhibitions and publications that seeks to prove costume's place in our cultural regard and in our aesthetic esteem with an argument that is as opulent as it is intellectual, as controversial as it is indisputable, and as iconoclastic as it is self-evident. If we can pose costume's self-awareness and significant mediation between zones of private and public expression, costume becomes more than feint or frivole. Costume is indispensable in the negotiation of human behavior and substantive as an art form.

Richard Martin and Harold Koda